Amazing Amber

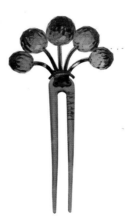

Andrew Ross and Alison Sheridan

with photographs by
Neil McLean and Bill Crighton

Amazing Amber

Exhibition:
10 May to 8 September 2013

National Museum of Scotland
Chambers Street
Edinburgh EH1 1JF

www.nms.ac.uk

First published in 2013 by
NMS Enterprises Limited – Publishing
a division of NMS Enterprises Limited
National Museums Scotland
Chambers Street, Edinburgh EH1 1JF

www.nms.ac.uk

Text and images:
© National Museums Scotland 2013, unless otherwise credited

The moral rights of Andrew Ross and Alison Sheridan
to be identified as the authors of this book have been
asserted by them in accordance with the Copyright,
Designs and Patents Act 1988.

British Library Cataloguing in Publication Data
A catalogue record for this book
is available from the British Library.

ISBN: 978 1 905267 79 8

Cover design: Mark Blackadder
Cover image and title page: Mexican amber contain-
    ing a wasp (see pages 6–7); faceted natural amber
    and tortoiseshell hair ornament (see page 33)
Publication format:
    NMS Enterprises Limited – Publishing
Printed and bound in the United Kingdom by
    ARC Printing Ltd, West Calder

For a full listing of NMS Enterprises Limited –
Publishing titles and related merchandise:

www.nms.ac.uk/books

Contents

Foreword

The diversity of the collections at National Museums Scotland is one of its strengths; the collections range across the Natural World, Science and Technology, Art and Design, Scottish History and Archaeology, and World Cultures. This means that we have a fantastic resource to draw on for exhibitions and we can make connections across the different subjects. This is what we have done for the exhibition 'Amazing Amber'.

Found all over the world, amber, fossilised tree resin, can vary widely in appearance and has many different uses. Our collections feature pieces from across the globe, from Borneo to the Baltic, from Sicily to Scotland. Used for centuries as a decorative artefact, amber was also treasured for its perceived magical powers, crafted into charms and amulets to heal and ward off evil spirits. The exhibition and book draw together a spectacular range of amber specimens and objects from our own and other important collections.

In addition, amber has the capacity to preserve life from millions of years ago in an astonishing detailed form and offers scientists a rich vein of research. The beautiful photographs, which are such an important part of this book, demonstrate this well.

This book, like the exhibition, gives you an insight into a fascinating subject and into the range of our collections. We thank all those who have made it possible.

Jane Carmichael
Director of Collections
NATIONAL MUSEUMS SCOTLAND

Opposite: Piece of Mexican amber
Length 60 mm

INTRODUCTION

Amazing Amber

Amber formed from resin that oozed out of cracks in the bark of trees millions of years ago. Sometimes the sticky resin captured insects and other organic matter. Left to harden and then buried in sediments, the amber endured, capturing an ancient moment in time.

Amber has been picked up and treasured by humans since prehistory and has often been worn as a symbol of power and status. Scotland is no exception as it has been worn here for over 5500 years and has even been found in archaeological sites as far north as the Orkney Islands. Amber artefacts provide interesting insights into ancient trade routes and the movements of individuals.

Amber is found all over the world, though only a few deposits are mined commercially. Amber has mostly been used to make jewellery. However, it has also been carved into a variety of items, such as religious altar-pieces, and has been put to more practical uses, such as mouth-pieces for tobacco pipes. Amber is truly a versatile material. Its value has led to a proliferation of fake amber-coloured imitation materials being produced over the past century.

Amber is famous for its animal and plant inclusions, particularly insects which, due to amber's unique properties, have been perfectly preserved for many millions of years. These inclusions provide a unique window to the past.

**Opposite:
Mexican amber
containing a wasp**

This large piece of Mexican amber shows the variety of shades that amber can be, from yellow to brown. The wasp trapped inside must have flown too near the sticky resin mass and got stuck.

Length 140 mm

What is Amber?

Amber is fossilised tree resin. Plants produce resin for defence; its antibacterial properties prevent disease and its stickiness gums up the jaws of insects that are trying to gnaw or burrow into bark. Some trees, such as certain pines, produce a lot of resin that seeps out of cracks in the bark and runs down their trunks.

Amber forms over millions of years. Resin first hardens into a substance called copal and chunks of copal get buried in soil and sediments. Over millions of years the copal slowly hardens into amber. Any insects or other inclusions that were stuck in the resin are perfectly preserved.

Opposite:
Tree oozing resin

This photograph shows a Monkey Puzzle tree oozing resin. Bark chips are clearly stuck in it.

Photograph by Emma Ross, taken at the Royal Botanic Garden, Edinburgh

---

Below: Flow planes

This piece of Baltic amber contains many layers that have built up by successive flows of resin. Insects are trapped within them.

Length 65 mm

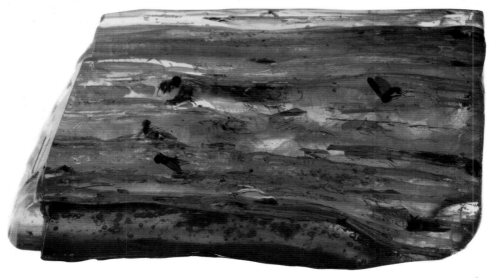

Copal

Copal from East Africa and Colombia is produced by the legume tree *Hymenaea*. Fresh pieces of East African copal are clear and light yellow, and often contain insects. Pieces that have been buried in the soil for thousands of years develop a distinctive pitted texture known as 'goose skin'. This texture can be ground away and polished to reveal any inclusions. With time, the surface starts to crack (craze) and the insects become harder to see.

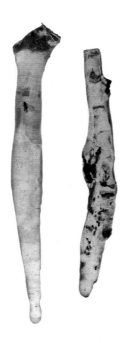

Colombian copal can also contain many kinds of insects, although often large, uniformly transparent lumps occur that usually contain only one species of termite. These large lumps formed within the cavities of hollow trees and probably took a long time to harden.

New Zealand copal is produced by the Kauri Pine, *Agathis australis*, and known as Kauri Gum. Very few insects live on Kauri Pines, so natural inclusions are rare. In the 19th century Kauri Gum was dug out of the ground for use in the varnish trade by 'gum diggers'. Many trees were chopped down and the remaining living trees are protected. There is no ready source of fresh copal, so specimens are usually old with a cracked (crazed) surface.

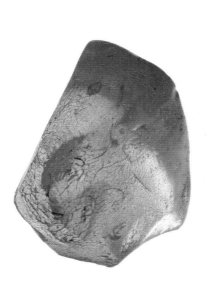

11

Where is Amber from?

Most of the world's amber comes from the Baltic region of northern Europe, but amber is found all over the world. Some rich deposits are mined commercially, particularly for the jewellery trade. Smaller deposits are mostly of scientific interest, especially amber that contains insects and other inclusions.

The oldest amber that contains inclusions comes from Italy and is from the Triassic Period (230 million years old). Most amber deposits are from the Cretaceous (66–145 million years old) and Tertiary (2.5–66 million years old) periods. Jurassic amber from Lebanon (145–157 million years old) is also known, but no inclusions have been found.

In the United Kingdom, Baltic amber is washed up on the east coast. It does, however, have its own native amber, but this is very rare. Evidence includes microscopic pieces of amber from Scotland (about 300 million years old), pieces from East Sussex (140 m.y.) and the Isle of Wight (125 m.y.), chalk deposits in England (100 m.y.), and clay deposits in Dorset and London (both about 50 m.y.). Pieces from the Isle of Wight have yielded a few insects and a spider.

Opposite and below: Amber pebbles from Fife, Scotland

These Baltic amber pebbles were washed up on the coast of Fife and have been cut and polished.

Opposite: From St Andrews, height 70 mm
Below, left: From St Andrews, lenth 50 mm
Below, right: From Elie, length 55 mm

Cretaceous Amber

Lebanese amber

Many localities in Lebanon are now known for amber, ranging from 94 to 157 million years ago. A whole variety of different colours occur, including fluorescent forms. A rich insect fauna is known which is 115 to 140 million years old. The chips shown here are from Hammana.

Length of largest chip 25 mm

Cretaceous Amber

Burmese amber

Amber has been mined in northern Burma for at least 2000 years. Much of it was exported to China where it was used for ornate carvings. Fresh out of the ground, Burmese amber is yellow or amber-coloured and darkens to red with age. Inclusions are common. A brown cloudy form known as root amber is also known. Recent scientific studies date Burmese amber at 99 million years old.

Length 30 mm

Spanish amber

There are now 120 known localities of amber in Spain, ranging in age from 66 to 235 million years old. Nine localities have yielded inclusions; most were discovered in the past two decades from Peñaccerada, El Soplao and San Just (between 94 and 113 million years old). This piece of amber, in three parts, is from San Just.

Length of largest piece 70 mm

French amber

There are over 70 recorded localities for amber from France, although most of the records are old. Amber from the Aquitaine and Paris regions dates to between 53 and 100 million years old. Studies of amber collected in France since the 1990s have yielded many inclusions. The pieces shown here are from Archingeay (left) and Le Quesnoy (right).

Lengths 30 mm

Tertiary Amber

Romanian amber

This example of dark red/brown amber, with the mineral name Schraufite, is from Vama in the Bukovina region. Schraufite is less common than the Rumanite variety, which comes from the Buzau region. Its exact age is uncertain.

Length 65 mm

Chinese amber

Most historical pieces of amber from China are actually Burmese amber. China does have its own amber deposits, although most are small and pieces are only used in traditional Chinese medicine. The best known Chinese amber comes from Fushun in Liaoning Province and contains inclusions. It was found as a by-product of coal-mining, which has now stopped. Fushun amber is about 50 million years old.

Length 30 mm

Sicilian amber

Sicilian amber dates from between 23 and 34 million years old. It is very rare today, but is well known for its bright fluorescing colours (including green and blue). This, however, fades with time as the amber oxidises, so old pieces are now amber to dark red in colour.

Length 40 mm

Tertiary Amber

South-east Asian amber

Amber comes from the Sabah and Sarawak regions of Malaysia, and the Kalimantan region of Indonesia, on the island of Borneo. Malaysian pieces are generally red/brown and translucent, but yellow copal pieces also occur in Sabah. More recently, fluorescent blue pieces have been found in Kalimantan and on the Indonesian island of Sumatra.

Sabah amber is between 12 and 16 million years old and Sarawak amber is probably similar in age. Some Kalimantan amber is 7 million years old, although the age of the blue amber is not known. Inclusions occur in the Malaysian pieces – however, no inclusions have yet been recorded from Kalimantan or Sumatra.

Above: Blue Kalimantan amber
Length 70 mm

Left: Sarawak amber
Length 140 mm

Tertiary Amber

Baltic amber

Baltic amber is between 28 and 38 million years old and is the best known amber. It comes in a wide colour range – from white, through yellow, amber, orange and red to black (yellow and amber are the most common colours). These can oxidise to orange and even red with time, though the red form is very rare. Black amber contains a high concentration of bark fragments, which came from the tree that produced it – an extinct conifer.

Baltic amber can be transparent or cloudy – the cloudiness is formed by millions of microscopic air bubbles. The transparent form often contains inclusions, including clusters of tiny hairs that came from the flowers of oak trees. These are a good sign of genuine Baltic amber.

Baltic amber comes from the Blue Earth deposit which runs underneath the Baltic Sea – amber is washed out of it by storms and can end up on beaches. Commercial amber mining began in about 1850 by the Stantien & Becker company and Baltic amber is still mined today – mainly in Kaliningrad, Russia.

Below: Bone amber

This polished piece of cloudy white Baltic amber also has transparent patches.

Length 55 mm

**Below, left:
Amber with crust**

This broken raw piece of Baltic amber has a dark oxidised crust.

Length 70 mm

Fresh transparent amber

This lemon-yellow colour is the natural colour of fresh Baltic amber. With time it will oxidise and darken to a more familiar amber colour.

Length 50 mm

Yellow cloudy amber

This piece of Baltic amber, with an unusually bright yellow colour, is part of a large pebble that has been broken.

Length 110 mm

Orange cloudy amber

This polished piece of cloudy Baltic amber has oxidised to an orange/brown colour.

Length 75 mm

Tertiary Amber

Dominican and Mexican amber

Dominican amber (from the Dominican Republic) and Mexican amber were produced by the legume tree *Hymenaea*, the same type of tree that produced East African and Colombian copal. These ambers are usually transparent, varying from yellow to orange, even within one piece. Fluorescent green and blue forms also exist. With time, however, these colours fade away due to oxidation. Both are well-renowned for their diverse insect and other inclusions and are 15–20 million years old. Mexican amber often contains parallel cracks formed from tectonic pressure.

Raw amber

This fractured piece of raw Mexican amber is still in its sandstone matrix.

Length 290 mm

Below: Dominican amber

Length 85 mm

Red Mexican amber
Length 65 mm

_____

Green Mexican amber
Length 40 mm

_____

Cloudy Mexican amber
Length 40 mm

_____

Blue Mexican amber
Length 65 mm

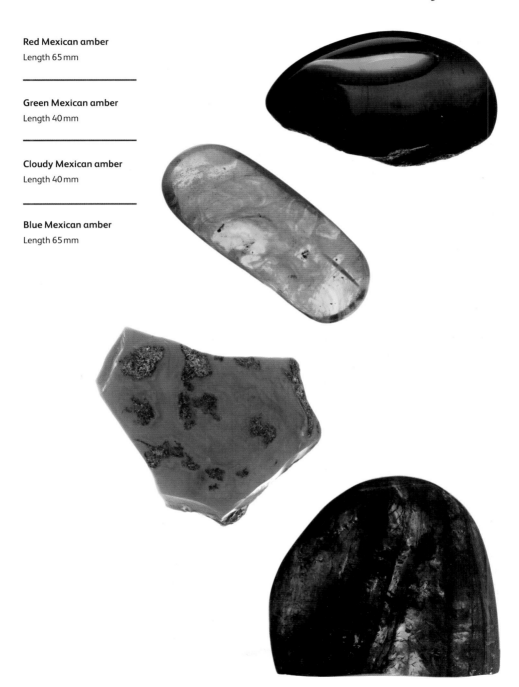

Balmashanner necklace

This necklace, comprising 25 graded amber beads and 5 of cannel coal or shale, came from a Late Bronze Age (about 8th century BC) hoard in Angus. This hoard also included 7 gold-covered hair-rings and 14 bronze bangles and bracelets. The amber is believed to have travelled far – first from Denmark to Ireland, where it was made into the necklace, and then to Scotland, as part of a wide trading network.

Diameter of largest bead 25 mm

Amber
in Scotland's Past

Amber has been used in Scotland for over 5500 years. Treasured as a rare and beautiful substance, it has been worn by wealthy and powerful people at different times in the past to show off their status. Because of its special properties – it is warm to the touch, can be burned, appears to glow in sunlight, and when rubbed generates static electricity – amber has also been credited with special powers, to protect from evil and to cure illnesses. People have therefore used it as an amulet or charm.

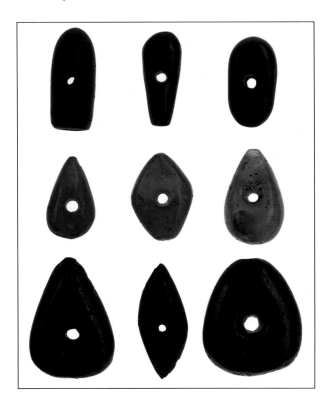

Left: Battle axehead-shaped beads

These amber and jet beads, shaped like miniature battle axeheads, probably date to around 1800 BC. They are unique and the necklace they formed would have been a high-status possession. They were reportedly found in a burial mound in Lanark-shire.

Longest amber bead 22 mm

Below: Bead from Early Bronze Age grave

This tiny bead, probably made from a pebble washed up on the east Scottish coast, comes from the grave of an important man who was buried with fancy archery gear. From Culduthel, Inverness, and dated to around 2100 BC.

Length 10 mm

Knowes of Trotty grave goods

These spectacular objects of amber and gold, around 4000 years old, are from the grave of a very important individual buried at the Knowes of Trotty, in Orkney.

The amber had probably made an amazing journey, first from Denmark to the Stonehenge area in southern England, where it was made into the necklace and ornaments, and then up to Orkney. Their owner – probably a woman – may have travelled from Orkney to Stonehenge to take part in the mid-winter solstice ceremonies there. Her cremated remains were found beside the objects.

Right: Beads and plates

From an old, worn amber 'spacer plate' necklace.

Width of rectangular spacer plate 43 mm
Illustration by Marion O'Neil

Below and opposite: Prismatic and hook-shaped ornaments

For a cape or gown.

Length of hook-shaped pieces 30 mm

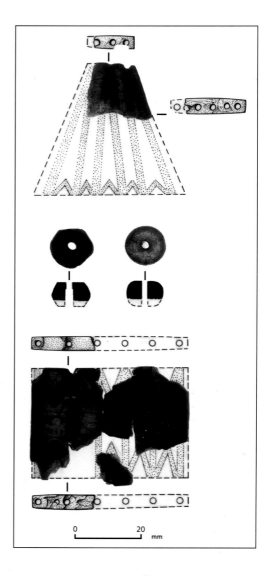

Above: Gold foil covers

Four domed ornaments that had probably been worn on the cape or gown.

Diameter of most complete disc 76 mm

Right: Artist's reconstruction

Showing how the Knowes of Trotty objects may have been worn.

Illustration by Marion O'Neil

Aristocratic dress accessories

In Early Medieval Scotland, amber-inlaid jewellery was a sign of high status. Between AD 700 and 900 it was often used in Scotland and Ireland to embellish items to fasten aristocratic clothing. Even the tiniest studs of amber, or fragments of brooch-pins with amber insets, were precious.

Dunipace brooch-pin

This pin, made of gilded silver, with amber insets and panels of interlace design featuring tail-biting creatures, was found at Dunipace, Stirling. It dates to the 8th century AD. This had been a prized possession because most brooch-pins at the time were made of bronze.

Length 130 mm

Westness brooch-pin

This pin, made of gilded silver, with insets of amber and red glass and panels of gold filigree, was found in the 9th-century grave of a Viking woman in Orkney. This particularly fine brooch had originally been made up to a century earlier, and it may have been stolen during a Viking raid in Scotland or Ireland, or else given to a Viking as a gift.

Length 205 mm

Rosemarkie pin

This bone pin with amber insets came from Rosemarkie, north of Inverness. Although simple in design, this pin was nevertheless a prestigious object thanks to its precious inlaid amber studs.

Length 40 mm

Warding off evil

In Scottish folklore, amber was believed to have a miraculous ability to ward off evil and to heal illnesses, especially those connected with eyesight. Strings of 'lammer-beads' were traditionally used to protect children and unbaptised babies against evil, and by adults as a cure for sore eyes. The name comes from the French word for amber – *l'ambre*. The amber charms from the west of Scotland are actually 2800-year-old Late Bronze Age beads that must have seemed miraculous when discovered around the 17th or 18th century AD.

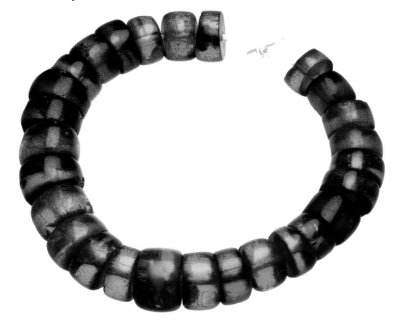

Left: Late Bronze Age bead used as a charm

This ancient bead, made around 800 BC, was used as a charm on the Isle of Skye during the 19th century and earlier. It was rubbed on the eyelids of a person with failing sight, in the belief that the amber would cure them.

Diameter 17 mm

Above: String of 'lammer-beads'

This was displayed in the Glasgow International Exhibition of 1888.

Largest bead diameter 20 mm

Four Late Bronze Age amber beads, used as a charm

These ancient beads were used by the Macdonalds of Glencoe as a charm against blindness. These beads probably came originally from a necklace like the one found at Balmashanner (see page 22).

Largest diameter 25 mm

Cattle charm

This amber pebble, on a silver chain, would have been dipped in the drinking water of sick cattle, in the belief that it would cure them. A spell would have been chanted as the pebble entered the water. The inscription on the silver disc reads, 'A gift from Angus Macdonald, Bridge of Coe, to H.McC. 1845'.

Length 90 mm

Amber Jewellery

Amber has been used to make jewellery for thousands of years. It is easily worked and the variety of colours and forms of amber make it a very versatile and beautiful material for makers and designers. For centuries, amber was an expensive, high status material, worn only by the élite. Today it is widely available and more affordable.

In Europe most of the amber used in jewellery is from the Baltic region. Freshly mined Baltic amber is yellow, though heat treatments are often used to turn it darker. Small amber chips can be pressed together or even embedded in plastic.

The unique appearance and high value of amber jewellery has led to many forms of imitation – using a wide variety of different materials – from glass to polystyrene. Sometimes it is easy to spot imitations; others are more subtle and require careful observation and testing to find out exactly what they are made of.

> Kate, eat apace; – And now, my honey love,
> Will we return unto thy father's house;
> And revel it as bravely as the best,
> With silken coats, and caps, and golden rings,
> With ruffs, and cuffs, and fardingals, and things;
> With scarfs, and fans, and double change of bravery,
> With amber bracelets, beads, and all this knavery.

William Shakespeare, *The Taming of the Shrew*, 1592

**Opposite, above:
Amber bracelet**

This beautiful bracelet is made from pieces of natural and heat-treated amber. The pieces that contain spangles (circular cracks) have been heat-treated to varying degrees.

Diameter 80 mm

**Opposite, below:
Contemporary amber ring**

The maker of this ring won a Design Award at the Amberif International Amber Fair in Gdansk in 2012. It is made from cylinders of natural and heat-treated amber set in a rubber mount, with a magnetic ring.

Length 60 mm

Natural amber

Natural amber has not been artificially altered in any way. Freshly mined Baltic amber is yellow, but gets darker in colour and develops surface cracks or 'crazes' as it ages. Natural Baltic amber also comes in a cloudy form – this does not darken or craze as much as transparent amber.

Left: Natural amber necklace

This is made from freshly mined natural Baltic amber. With time it will darken to the more familiar amber colour.

Largest bead diameter 20 mm

Below: Natural amber pendant

This is made from freshly mined natural cloudy Baltic amber.

Length 45 mm
Emma Ross Collection

Faceted natural amber necklace

This is an old necklace as demonstrated by the crazing (fine cracking) on its surface and it has darkened with time. All the facets are made by hand. It entered the collections of the museum in 1886.

Largest bead diameter 25 mm

Inset: Faceted natural amber and tortoiseshell hair ornament

The beautiful hair ornament is in the Art Nouveau style.

Length 120 mm

Heat-treated amber jewellery

Most of the amber jewellery you see in shops in the United Kingdom has been heat-treated to change its colour and produce
circular cracks called 'spangles' or 'scales'. Some people think
that these cracks are natural inclusions, but this is incorrect. The
amber is treated in an autoclave, a pressure cooker that essen-
tially cooks the amber to varying degrees. Cloudy amber can be
clarified by adding vegetable oils. Some refer to heat-treated
amber as 'improved' amber, although it is a matter of personal
taste whether this process is considered as an improvement on
natural amber.

Heat-treated amber pendant

This pendant has been auto-
claved to make it darker and to
produce spangles.

Length 55 mm

**Yellow heart-shaped amber
pendant**

This pendant has been auto-
claved with an inert gas to
produce the spangles but not
darken it.

Length 23 mm

Green amber pendant

This pendant has been auto-
claved to produce the spangles;
then the back has been painted
black to produce the green
colour. Burning the back of
amber produces a similar effect.

Length 50 mm

Right: Polybern bracelet

You can clearly see the chips of amber in the plastic.

Diameter 80 mm

Below: Pressed amber necklace

This necklace is more brown than it would be if natural.

Largest bead diameter 15 mm

Pressed amber and polybern

Pressed, or reconstituted amber, is made from fusing chips of amber or ground-up amber together using heat and pressure. Sometimes plastic or copal is added to the mix. Pressed amber is produced as cylinders or slabs which can be carved and shaped. Where chips are used, it is possible to see the irregular joins between chips, but it is harder to distinguish ground up amber from natural or heat-treated amber.

Polybern is a 'halfway stage' between real and fake amber. It is made from chips of real amber, embedded in polyester resin. This method of making jewellery and other objects was widespread in Germany in the 1980s.

Glass and natural semi-precious stones

Visually, glass and natural silica (agate, carnelian and citrine) can look very much like amber, but on examination it is easy to tell them apart as they are heavy, cold to the touch and much harder than amber. Amber, on the other hand, is lighter, warm and can be scratched with a pin.

Left: Agate necklace
Largest bead width 15 mm

Below: Glass necklace
Bead width 13 mm

36

Plastics

A variety of different plastics has been used to fake amber over
the past 100 years or more, particularly Bakelite (phenolic resin),
celluloid, Galalith (casein), acrylic, polyester and polystyrene.
Plastic is sometimes mistaken for real amber because it has a
similar warm feel. A good test is the saturated saltwater test –
most plastics (except polystyrene) will sink, but real amber will
float. Plastic beads are very often all the same shape and colour,
or show mould lines or air bubbles in the centres of the thread
holes, indicating that they have been made in a mould, not by
hand. Some beads contain spangles or swirls of lighter or darker
plastic. You can also get composite plastic necklaces made from
a variety of different beads.

Chinese pressed amber bottle

China has a long tradition of carving amber, dating back at least 2000 years. Most of the amber used was from Burma. Burmese amber often has flaws and cracks filled with calcite, which makes it difficult to carve, so the Chinese developed a method of producing pressed amber. This allowed them to carve objects of any size rather than be restricted by the size of the piece of amber. This bottle is made from Baltic amber and is dated to the Qing Dynasty (18th century).

Height 240 mm

Decorative Amber

As amber is relatively soft and easily worked, it has been carved into a variety of different objects. Some of these objects are stunningly beautiful and have been made by skilled craftsmen. Some also have a function.

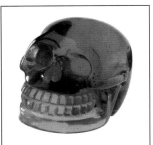

Left: Root amber snuff bottle

This snuff bottle was made in China, although the amber originally came from Burma. It dates to the Late Qing Dynasty (19th century).

Height 75 mm

Below, left: Carved skull

This piece of Mexican amber has been carved into a skull, probably for the tourist market rather than the Mexican Day of the Dead ceremony.

Length 55 mm

Below, right: Japanese amber netsuke

A netsuke is a carved toggle used to secure a medicine case or tobacco pouch hung from a sash. These toggles were carved into many different shapes and made from a number of different materials. This one is carved of amber from Kuji and is dated to the Edo period (19th century).

Length 50 mm

Religious carvings

These beautiful 17th-century carvings, showing religious scenes, are carved in the Italian style and probably came from the same workshop. They would have been used as altar-pieces in a domestic setting. They are made from Baltic amber.

Opposite: *The Rest on the Flight into Egypt with the Miracle of the Palm*

This beautiful carving is backed with the blue rock lapis lazuli. At this time this rock was very rare – it only came from Afghanistan and was extremely valuable.

Height 275mm
© Victoria and Albert Museum. Given by W. L. Hildburgh FSA.

Above: *The Baptism of Christ*

This amber carving was mounted on a copper alloy plate, coated with silver, which has since tarnished. Unfortunately it has not survived as well as the above piece, and has suffered some damage which has been crudely repaired.

Height 240mm

Cutlery

Cutlery with amber handles is first recorded in the 14th century, but probably originated before then. Examples with the most ornate amber handles were made in the 17th and 18th centuries, mostly in Poland and Prussia, and used for special occasions.

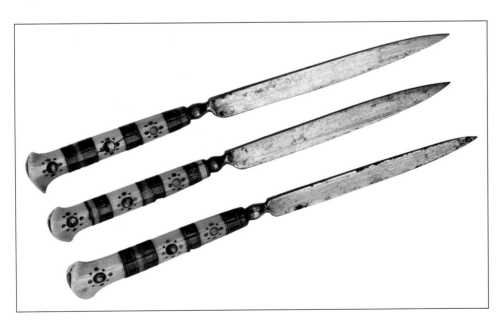

Tobacco smoking

Meerschaum clay pipes were often made with amber mouth-pieces as this gave a smoother smoke and prevented the clay pipe sticking to the lips. Cigarette and cheroot holders also often had mouth-pieces made of amber. Pressed amber and Bakelite were also used.

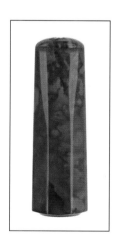

Amber pipe mouth-piece

This Baltic amber mouth-piece would have been originally attached to a Meerschaum pipe.

Length 65 mm

Art Deco cigarette case

This cigarette case is adorned with rectangular pieces of Baltic amber. This is typical of the Art Deco style which was popular in the 1930s and '40s.

Length 80 mm

Above: Churchwarden pipe with amber mouth-piece

This long pipe with its Baltic amber mouth-piece is a copy of a polished Dutch pipe. It is dated to the 19th century.

Length 450 mm

Fakes

Amber is often faked, not only in jewellery but also carvings and inclusions. Sometimes the fakes are so good that they even fool experts. Plastic is commonly used to fake amber, with large inclusions embedded within. Glass is sometimes mistaken for amber, but is not used to deliberately fake amber – you cannot embed inclusions in it.

Japanese netsuke

This netsuke was registered in the National Museums Scotland collections as amber. However, when it was recently tested, it was found to be made of celluloid.

Height 40 mm

Scorpion in plastic

Scorpions are very rare in amber, although fakes in plastic are common.

Length 65 mm

Bug in plastic

This shield bug in plastic has its legs and antennae neatly spread out, which does not happen with real inclusions.

Length 45 mm

Copal – hardened tree resin – is often passed off as amber, although it is usually too soft for jewellery. Copal often contains natural inclusions, which belong to more advanced species than you get in amber. It can be melted down to embed inclusions, although these faked inclusions are often large and too perfect to be true. Copal pieces can easily be tested with a drip of alcohol, which makes the surface sticky. Recently amber forgers have found a way to harden and darken copal to make it look like amber, which is very difficult to tell apart from the real thing and a big threat to the amber trade.

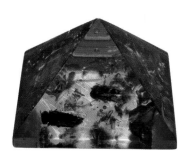

Polybern pyramid containing two bees

Polybern is made from chips of Baltic amber embedded in poly-ester. It is often sold as amber and sometimes has faked inclusions, such as the two bees seen here.

45 mm square
Alison Sheridan Collection

Madagascan copal pendant

This pendant has been heat-treated and was being sold as amber. The element that gave it away was the fly, as it is of a kind that is not found in amber.

Length 25 mm

Heart-shaped amulet

This intriguing object was said to have been found in Aberdeen-shire and thought to be amber and old. It was purchased by the Museum in 1889. However, recent examination and testing has revealed that it is actually East African copal. It was probably brought to the United Kingdom for the varnish trade, or could have been a curio brought back from Africa by a travelling Scot.

Length 50 mm

Insects
and other Inclusions

Amber has a unique capacity to preserve tiny insects and other delicate organisms for millions of years – these are known as inclusions.

Animal and plant inclusions are often perfectly preserved – from the facets of the eyes and the hairs on the legs to the stamens of flowers. They are an extraordinary source of information about the history of life on Earth.

Amber has preserved many thousands of species that would otherwise have remained unknown. They can be directly compared to living species to trace how they have evolved through time. Sometimes inclusions reveal evidence of behaviour or even interactions between different organisms – moments captured forever.

It is manifest, that Flyes, Spiders, Ants, or the like small creatures, falling by chance into Amber, or the Gums of Trees, and so finding a buriall in them, doe never after corrupt, or rot, although they be soft and tender Bodies. ... Entombed in a more stately Monument than Kings are, to be laid up for Eternitie.

Sir Francis Bacon, *History of Life and Death*,
first English edition, 1638

Opposite:
Gall midge

This is the first gall midge (Diptera: Cecidomyiidae) known from Chinese (Fushun) amber.

Length of wing 1 mm

Burmese amber inclusions

Burmese amber is 99 million years old, dating from the Cretaceous Period – when dinosaurs still roamed the Earth. The insects in Burmese amber are very varied and include many extinct groups of species, but also groups that are still very much alive today. Burmese amber has been studied for around 120 years and over 200 species have been named so far.

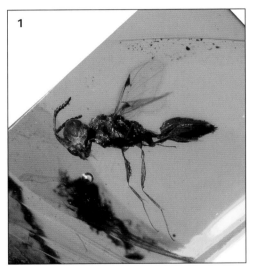

1

1. Extinct parasitic wasp

In the mid-1990s, studies of insects in Burmese amber shed new light on their likely age. The amber was previously dated to between 35 and 55 million years old, but the research showed that some of the inclusions belonged to extinct families only known from the Cretaceous Period, such as this parasitic wasp (Hymenoptera: Serphitidae). A study published in 2012 dated the Burmese amber bed as 99 million years old.

Length, from tips of head to abdomen, 2 mm

2. Biting midge

The notorious Highland midge is not just one species, but several closely related species of biting midges (Diptera: Ceratopogonidae). Female biting midges feed on the blood of many different kinds of animals – not just mammals, as some even feed on the blood of other insects, or nectar. Biting midges have been found in many different kinds of amber. This female has long pointed mouth-parts. What could it have fed on?

Length 1 mm

2

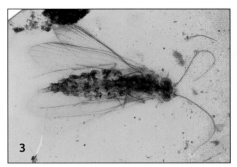

3. Caddisfly (Trichoptera: Psychomyiidae)

Length 2.5 mm

4. Woodlouse (Isopoda)

Length 3 mm

5. Planthopper nymph (Hemiptera: Fulgoroidea)

Length of piece 10 mm

6. Centipede (Chilopoda: Scolopendromorpha)

Length 9 mm

7. Ichneumon wasp (Hymenoptera: Ichneumonidae)

Length of wing 2.5 mm

8. Moth (Lepidoptera: Micropterigidae)

Length 2.5 mm

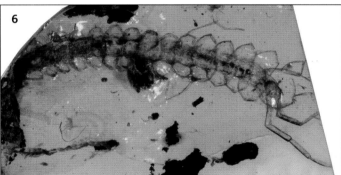

9. Scale insect (Hemiptera: Coccoidea)

Length 2.5 mm

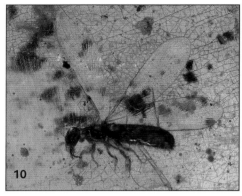

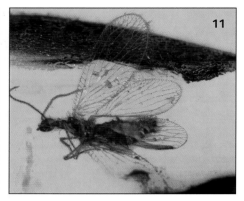

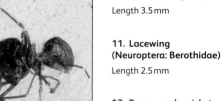

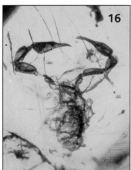

10. Termite (Isoptera)
Length 3.5 mm

11. Lacewing (Neuroptera: Berothidae)
Length 2.5 mm

12. Pygmy mole cricket (Orthoptera: Tridactylidae)
Length, excluding legs, 3 mm

13. Spider (Araneae: Archaeidae)
Length 2 mm

14. True bug (Hemiptera: Miridae)
Length 3 mm

15. Hairy millipede (Diplopoda: Synxenidae)
Length 2 mm

16. Pseudoscorpion (Pseudoscorpiones)
Length, excluding pincers, 2 mm

17. Fungus gnat (Diptera: Lygistorrhinidae)
Length 1.5 mm

1. Swarm of midges

You can sometimes find many individuals of the same species trapped in one piece of amber. Here you can see many midges (Diptera: Chironomidae) that were trapped while taking part in a mating swarm.

Length 2 mm

2. Rock crawler

This rock crawler is from a group that has features similar to praying mantises and stick insects. They were discovered in Baltic amber before they were found living today in Africa. In 2002, the group was named as a new order of insects, the Mantophasmatodea.

Length 4.5 mm

3. Dance fly

This dance fly (Diptera: Empididae) has long flat spines on its legs. It would have waved its spiny legs around to attract a mate.

Length 4 mm

Baltic amber inclusions

Baltic amber is 28–38 million years old and formed in a vast forest which spread over much of northern Europe. Some of the insects in Baltic amber have their closest relatives living today in south-east Asia, southern Africa and South America, demonstrating the dramatic migration of insect populations over long time periods. Baltic amber has been studied for over 300 years – thus far around 3000 species have been named.

4. Crane-flies (Diptera: Limoniidae)

Length of wings 5.5 mm

5. Lacewing larva (Neuroptera)

Length 6.5 mm

6. Flower stamens (Angiospermae)

Length 6 mm

7. Tumbling flower beetle (Coleoptera: Mordellidae)

Length 3 mm

8. Ants (Hymenoptera: Formicidae)

Length 2.5 mm

9. Cricket (Orthoptera: Ensifera)

Length 9 mm

10. Spider (Araneae: Tetragnathidae)

Length, excluding legs, 3 mm

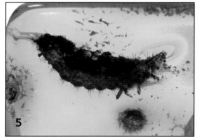

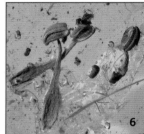

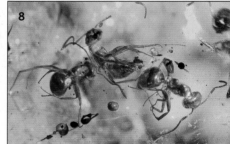

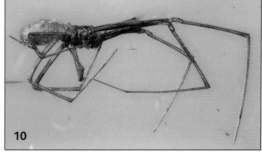

11. **Pseudoscorpion (Pseudo-scorpiones: Neobisiidae)**
Length 1.5 mm

12. **Moth (Lepidoptera)**
Length 6 mm

13. **Sawfly larva (Hymenoptera: Symphyta)**
Length 4.5 mm

14. **Cupedid beetle (Coleoptera: Cupedidae)**
Length 6.5 mm

15. **Long-legged fly (Diptera: Dolichopodidae)**
Length 4 mm

16. **Hoverfly (Diptera: Syrphidae)**
Length 6.5 mm

17. **Fungus gnat (Diptera: Sciaridae)**
Length 2.5 mm

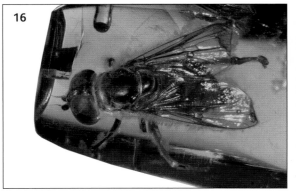

Mexican amber inclusions

Mexican amber is 15–20 million years old and formed in a tropical dry forest, close to a mangrove swamp. It has not received as much attention as some of the other kinds of amber. Even though it has been studied for the past 50 years, only about 100 species of insect have been named so far. Many of the specimens in the collections of National Museums Scotland are still to be studied in detail and could reveal fascinating new information.

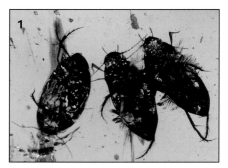

1. Water beetles

Aquatic animals in amber present a puzzle – how did they end up trapped in tree resin? Blobs of resin may have fallen into ponds and streams in the forest. Another possibility is epiphytes – plants which grow on tree branches, high up in the canopy of tropical forests. One group of epiphytes are the bromeliads, which have pools of water between their thick leaves. These pools support their own eco-system of aquatic life. It is possible to imagine blobs of resin dropping from the trees into bromeliad pools and these beetles (Coleoptera) swimming into them.

Length 4.5mm

2. Pseudoscorpion holding an ant

Pseudoscorpions (Pseudoscorpiones) are predators and this one is still holding on to an ant (Hymenoptera: Formicidae) that may have been its prey.

Length, excluding pincers, 2mm

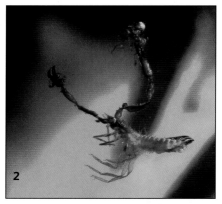

3. Giant termite

Mastotermes (Isoptera: Mastotermitidae) is the largest and most primitive termite living today. It is only native to Australia. Both fossils and preserved amber inclusions of *Mastotermes* have been found in several parts of the world, including southern England, showing that in the past *Mastotermes* existed much more widely. Termites are social insects with different castes that undertake different roles in the colony. Here is a winged adult that would have swarmed to try to start a new colony.

Length 32mm

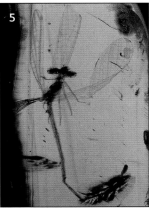

4. Snipe fly (Diptera: Rhagionidae)

Length 4 mm

5. Damselfly (Odonata: Zygoptera)

Width of head 4 mm

6. Fungus weevil (Coleoptera: Anthribidae)

Length 6 mm

7. Leaf of flowering plant (Angiospermae)

Length 17 mm

8. Cockroach (Blattodea: Ectobiidae)

Length 6 mm

9. Centipede (Chilopoda: Geophilomorpha)

Length of head 1 mm

10. Earwig (Dermaptera: Diplatyidae)

Length 10 mm

11. Liverwort (Jungermanniales)

Length 8 mm

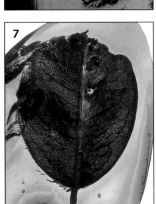

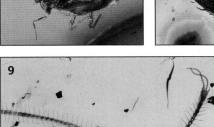

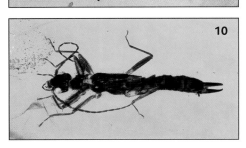

12. Flower (Angiospermae)

Width 3 mm

13. Leafhopper (Hemiptera: Cicadellidae) and scuttle fly (Diptera: Phoridae)

Length of leafhopper 6.5 mm

14. Assassin bug (Hemiptera: Reduviidae)

Length 9.5 mm

15. Plant or fungal structure shedding spores

Length 9 mm

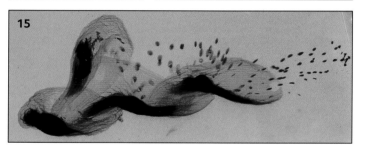

16. Planthopper (Hemiptera: Tropiduchidae)

Length 16 mm

17. Long-horn beetle (Coleoptera: Cerambycidae)

Length 12 mm

18. Moth (Lepidoptera)

Length 10 mm

1. Insects stuck to spider silk

Amber is amazing for preserving the most delicate of structures, such as parts of spiders' webs. Here you can see a tiny fairy fly (left, Hymenoptera: Mymaridae) and gall midge (right, Diptera: Cecidomyiidae) hanging from strands of spider silk.

Length of fairy fly 0.5 mm

---

2. Beetle with pseudoscorpion passenger

Pseudoscorpions (Pseudoscorpiones) cannot fly so hitch rides on flying insects by grabbing hold of them, a behaviour known as phoresy. This one is hanging on to a flat-footed beetle (Coleoptera: Platypodidae).

Length of beetle 3.5 mm

---

3. Ant carrying a scale insect

Ants (Hymenoptera: Formicidae) feed from the honeydew secretions of aphids (Hemiptera: Aphidoidea) and scale insects (Hemiptera: Coccoidea) and in turn protect them from predators. When some species of ants swarm, they take scale insects with them to start new colonies and have a ready food source, as can be seen here.

Length 2 mm

Dominican amber inclusions

Dominican amber is 15–20 million years old and formed in a tropical moist forest, similar to such forests living today. This environment supports the most number of species on land, and so a large variety are trapped in Dominican amber. Although this amber has only been studied for the past 50 years, over 400 species of insect have been named so far.

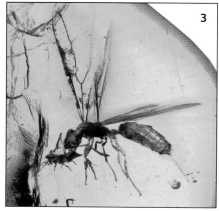

4. March fly (Diptera: Bibionidae)

Length 3 mm

5. Termites and their wings (Isoptera)

Length of piece 20 mm

6. Bethylid wasp (Hymenoptera: Bethylidae)

Length 3 mm

7. Earwig (Dermaptera)

Length 5 mm

8. Winged fruit of a flowering plant (Angiospermae: Polygonaceae)

Width 8.5 mm

9. Skeletonised leaf of a flowering plant (Angiospermae)

Width 12 mm

10. Bristletail (Archaeognatha: Machilidae)

Length, including tail, 9 mm

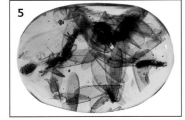

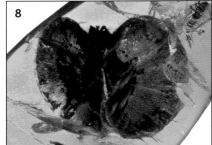

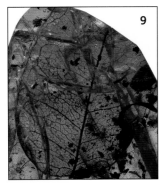

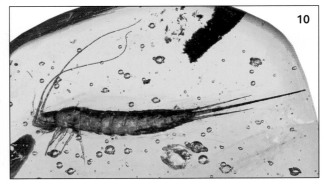

11

12

11. Scavenger fly (Diptera: Scatopsidae)

Length 2.5 mm

12. Bark-louse (Psocoptera: Psocidae)

Length 2.5 mm

13. Planthopper (Hemiptera: Cixiidae)

Length 4.5 mm

14. Braconid wasp (Hymenoptera: Braconidae)

Length 3.5 mm

15. Mushroom (Fungi)

Width 3 mm

16. Woodlouse (Isopoda)

Length 3 mm

17. Moth (Lepidoptera)

Length 6 mm

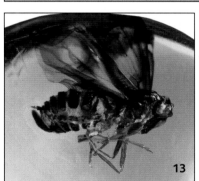

13

14

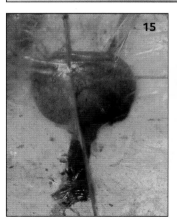

15

16

17

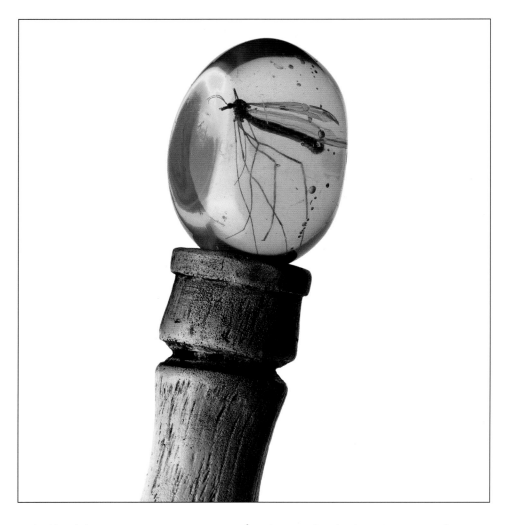

'Amber'-headed cane

This cane was the one used in *The Lost World*, the sequel to the film *Jurassic Park*. The plastic head contains a crane-fly (Diptera: Tipulidae), not a mosquito.

Height 240 mm
Courtesy of NBC Universal Archives & Collections

Opposite: Stingless bee in Dominican amber

The first claims of ancient insect DNA from amber were made by scientists in California in 1992. They claimed to have extracted DNA from specimens of this extinct species of bee (Hymenoptera: Apidae: *Proplebeia dominicana*). Stingless bees are very common in Dominican amber because they would have collected resin to make their nests. It is easy to imagine them getting trapped as they did this. Subsequent attempts to extract DNA from these bees by other scientists have failed.

Length 3 mm

DNA from Amber?

First screened in 1993, the blockbuster film *Jurassic Park* fired a new public interest in insects trapped in amber. The plot revolves around scientists bringing dinosaurs back to life, using DNA extracted from blood taken from mosquitoes trapped in amber.

Based on the best-selling book by Michael Crichton, *Jurassic Park* has some foundation in science. In the early 1990s, scientists in the United States of America claimed to have extracted insect DNA from insects in amber. However, DNA is a very unstable molecule and there was scepticism that it could survive millions of years. Other similar experiments since then have failed, indicating that the results from the first experiments were probably affected by contamination.

Below: Mosquito in East African copal

Mosquitoes (Diptera: Culicidae) do occur in amber, but they are very rare. Most 'mosquito' inclusions are actually fungus gnats. When *Jurassic Park* was first screened, there were no known examples of mosquitoes in amber from the age of the dinosaurs. Since then only two have been found – one in Canadian amber and the other in Burmese amber.

Length 3.5mm

Bibliography

Beck, C. and Shennan, S. 1991. *Amber in prehistoric Britain*. (Oxbow Books), 232 pp.

Causey, F. 2011. *Amber and the ancient world* (J. Paul Getty Museum, Los Angeles), 152 pp.

Clark, N. D. L. 2010. *Amber, Tears of the Gods* (Dunedin Academic Press Ltd), 118 pp.

Fraquet, H. 1987. *Amber* (Butterworths), 176 pp.

Grimaldi, D. A. 1996. *Amber, window to the past* (Harry N. Abrams), 216 pp.

Penney, D. (ed.) 2010. *Biodiversity of fossils in amber from the major world deposits* (Siri Scientific Press), 304 pp.

Penney, D. and D. I. Green 2011. *Fossils in amber, remarkable snapshots of prehistoric fossil life* (Siri Scientific Press), 215 pp.

Poinar, G. O. 1992. *Life in amber* (Stanford University Press), 350 pp.

Poinar, G. and R. Poinar 1994. *The quest for life in amber* (Helix Books), 219 pp.

Poinar, G. and R. Poinar 1999. *The amber forest, a reconstruction of a vanished world* (Princeton University Press), 239 pp.

Poinar, G. and R. Poinar 2008. *What bugged the dinosaurs?* (Princeton University Press), 264 pp.

Rice, P. C. 2006. *Amber, the Golden Gem of the Ages* (4th edition) (AuthorHouse), 436 pp.

Ross, A. J. 2010. *Amber, the Natural Time Capsule* (2nd edition) (London: Natural History Museum), 112 pp.

Salle, R. De. and D. Lindley 1998. *The science of Jurassic Park and the Lost World or, how to build a dinosaur* (Flamingo), 194 pp.

Trusted, M. 1985. *Catalogue of European ambers in the Victoria and Albert Museum* (London: Victoria and Albert Museum), 119 pp.

Weitschat, W. and W. Wichard 2002. *Atlas of plants and animals in Baltic amber* (Dr Friedrich Pfeil), 256 pp.

Williamson, G. C. 1932. *The book of amber* (Ernest Benn Ltd), 268 pp.

Acknowledgements

National Museums Scotland would like to thank the following individuals and institutions:

Neil McLean for the photography of the objects and Bill Crighton for the photography of the inclusions; the exhibition staff, curators and collections services staff of the Museum for all their hard work and assistance.

The Abbotsford Trust, Scott Anderson, Sir David Attenborough, Henrietta Lidchi, Natural History Museum (London), NBC Universal, Orkney Museum, Emma Ross, Alison Sheridan, and the Victoria and Albert Museum, for loans to the exhibition 'Amazing Amber'.

Sir David Attenborough, Janusz Fudala (Ambersafari), Doug Lundberg (amberica west), André Nel (Muséum national d'Histoire naturelle, Paris), Ted Pilecki (The Amber Centre), Bob Rontaler (Goldmajor Ltd), Jevgenij Semionov (Memelland Ltd), Ma Shilian (Fushun amber shop, Beijing), and Roland Torikian, for the donation of specimens.

Emma Ross for the image on p. 8; Marion O'Neil for the illustrations on pp. 24 and 25.

For help with identifying inclusions, or for supplying information about other objects, thanks are due to Dany Azar (Lebanese University), Hugh Cheape (Sabhal Mór Ostaig), Margaret Collinson (Royal Holloway and Bedford New College), Greg Edgecombe (Natural History Museum, London), Michael Engel (University of Kansas), Ed Jarzembowski (Nanjing Institute of Geology and Palaeontology), Mark Judson (Muséum national d'Histoire naturelle, Paris), Greg Kenicer (Royal Botanic Garden, Edinburgh), Rachel King (Bayerisches National Museum, Munich), Wieslaw Krzeminski (Institute of Systematics and Evolution of Animals, Krakow), Craig Macadam (Buglife), Steven Manchester (Florida Museum of Natural History), Wolfram Mey (Museum für Naturkunde, Berlin), David Penney (University of Manchester), Evgeny Perkovsky (Schmalhausen Institute of Zoology, Ukraine), Yuri Popov (Palaeontological Institute, Moscow), Alexandr Rasnitsyn (Palaeontological Institute, Moscow), Ryszard Szadziewski (University of Gdansk), Jacek Szwedo (Museum and Institute of Zoology, Warsaw) and Wilfried Wichard (University of Köln).

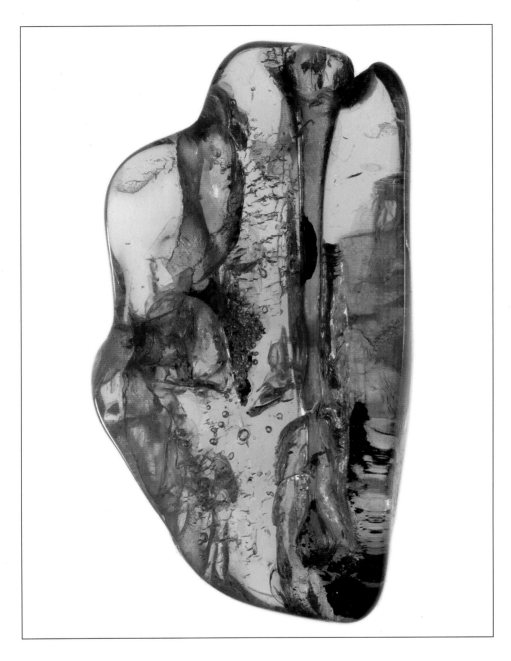

Stalactite in Baltic amber

Length of piece 40 mm